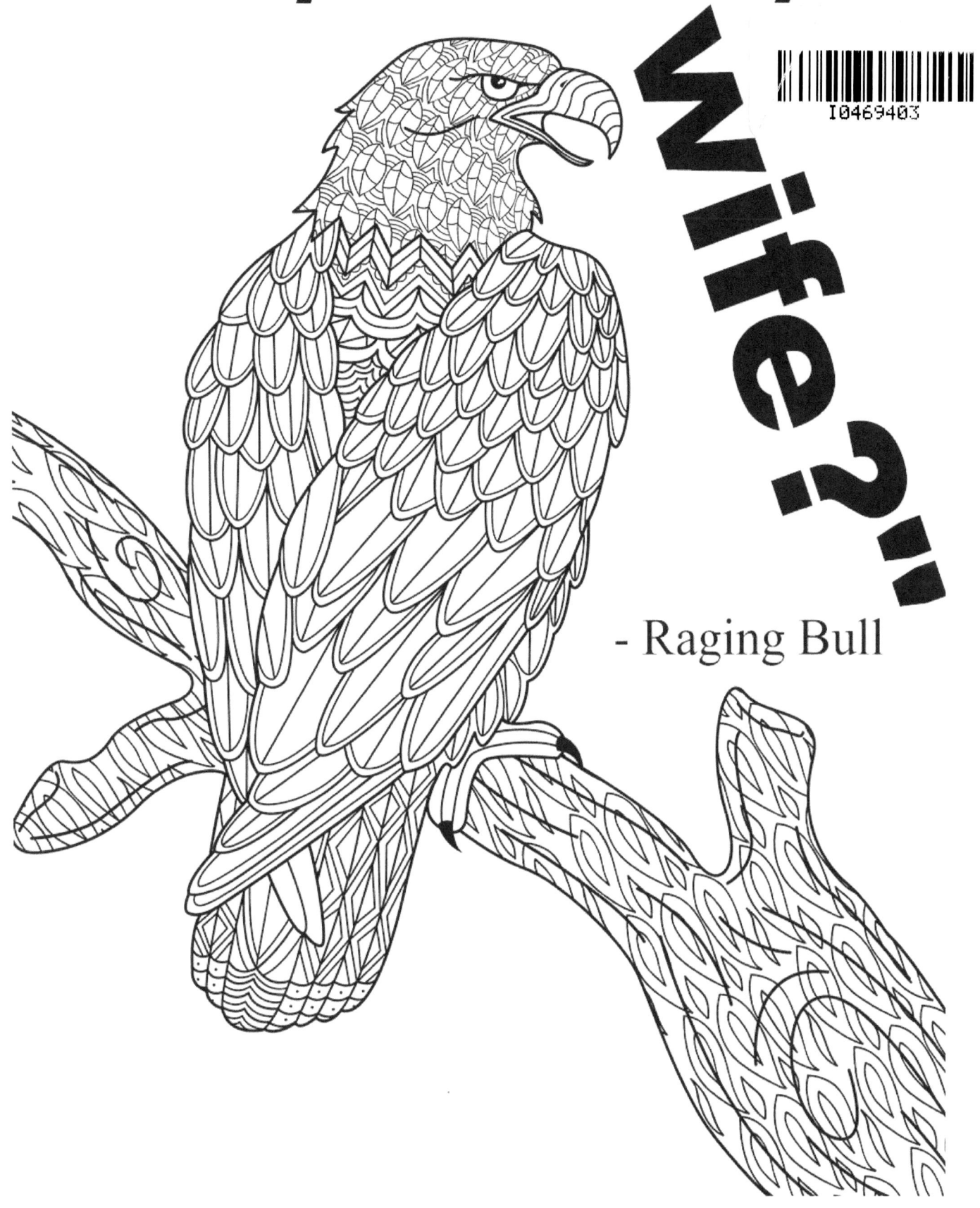

ISBN: 978-1530055296
Illustrated by:
Mandala & Caricature Illustration
Joshua Lazana Lagman and Jade Villaremo

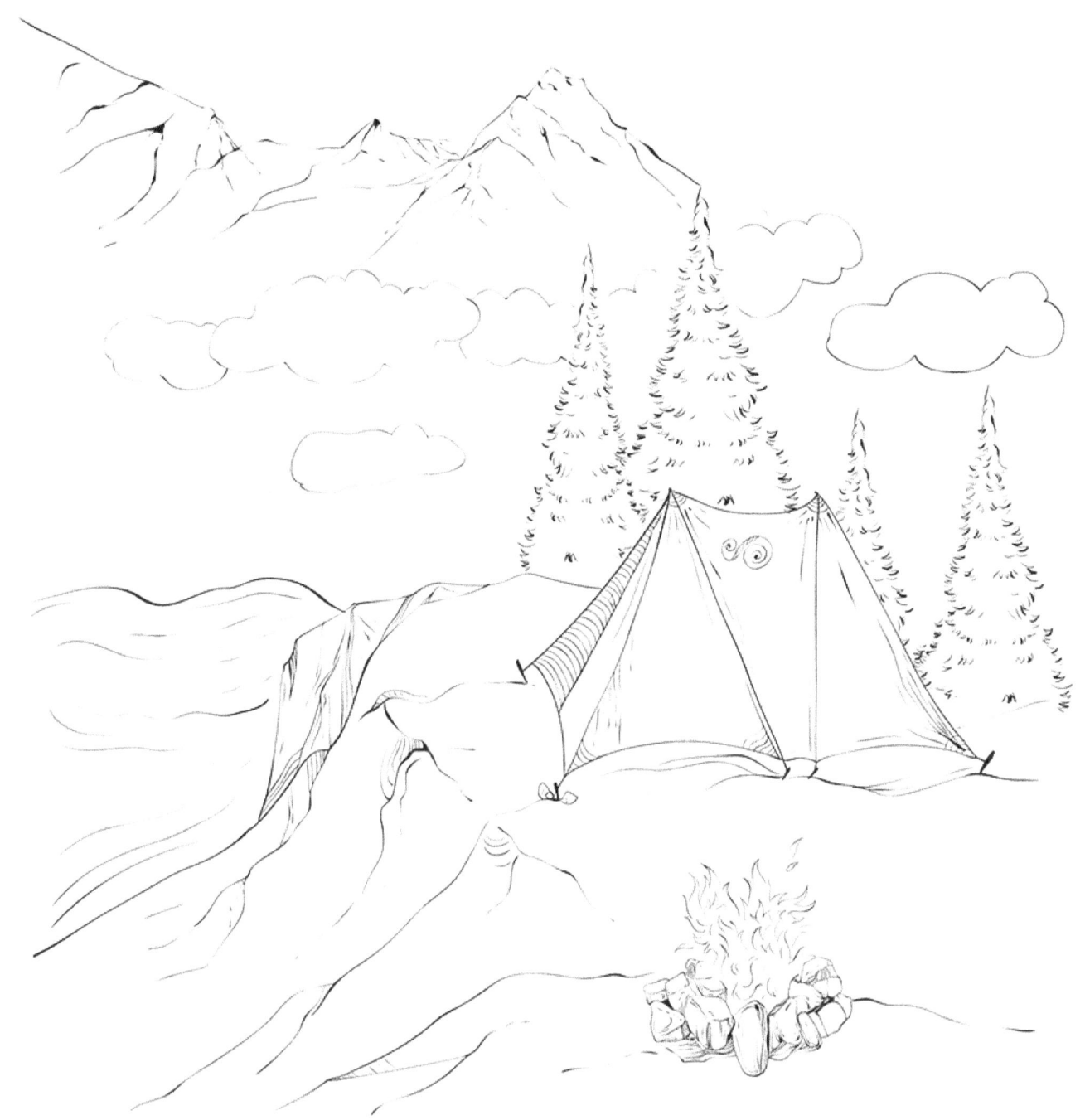

"Things are fucked up at the North Pole.
Mrs Claus caught me fucking her sister,
now I'm out on my ass."

– Willie (Billie Bob Thornton) in Bad Santa

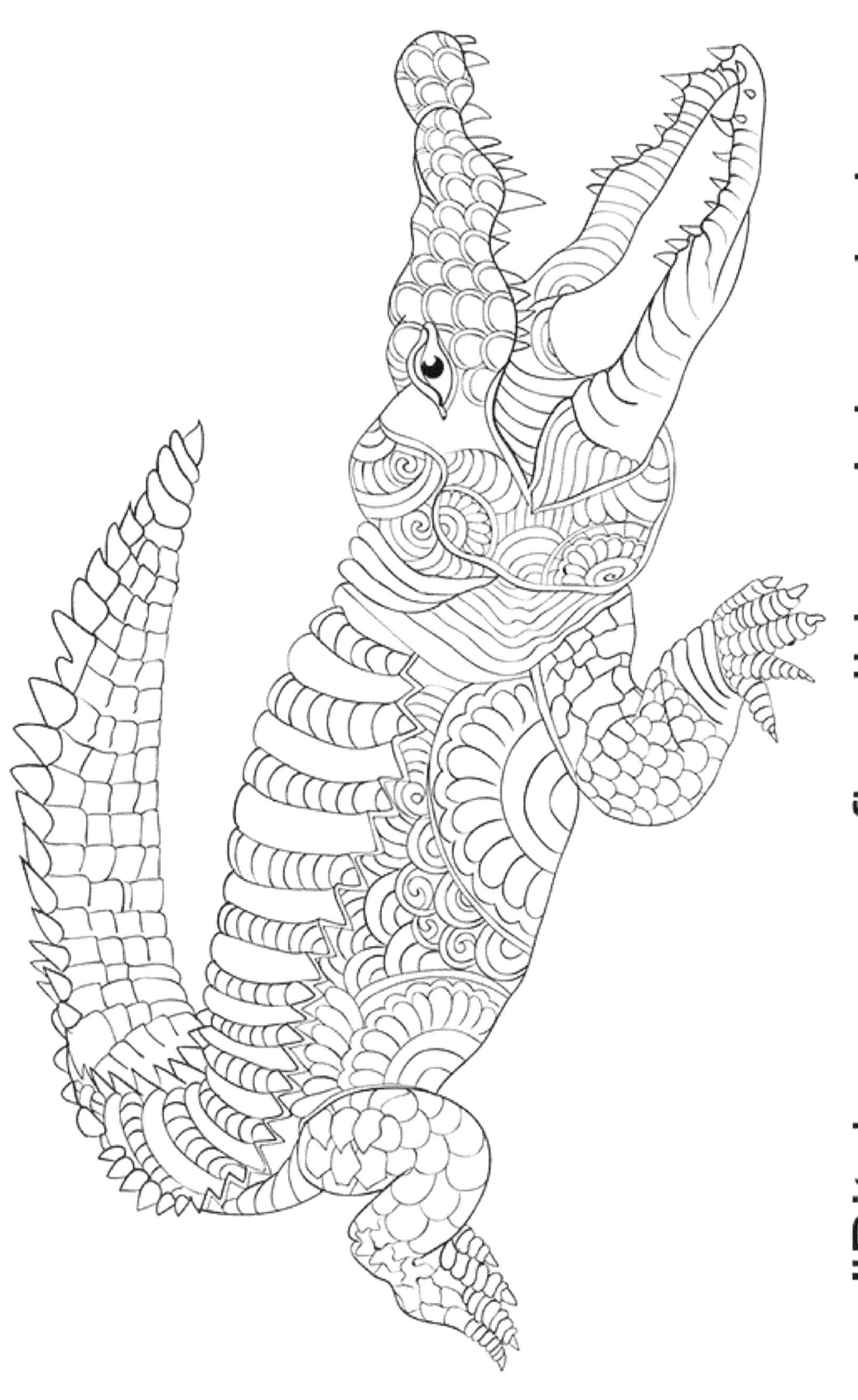

"Bitch was so fine I'd suck her dad-
dy's dick."

–Richard Pryor

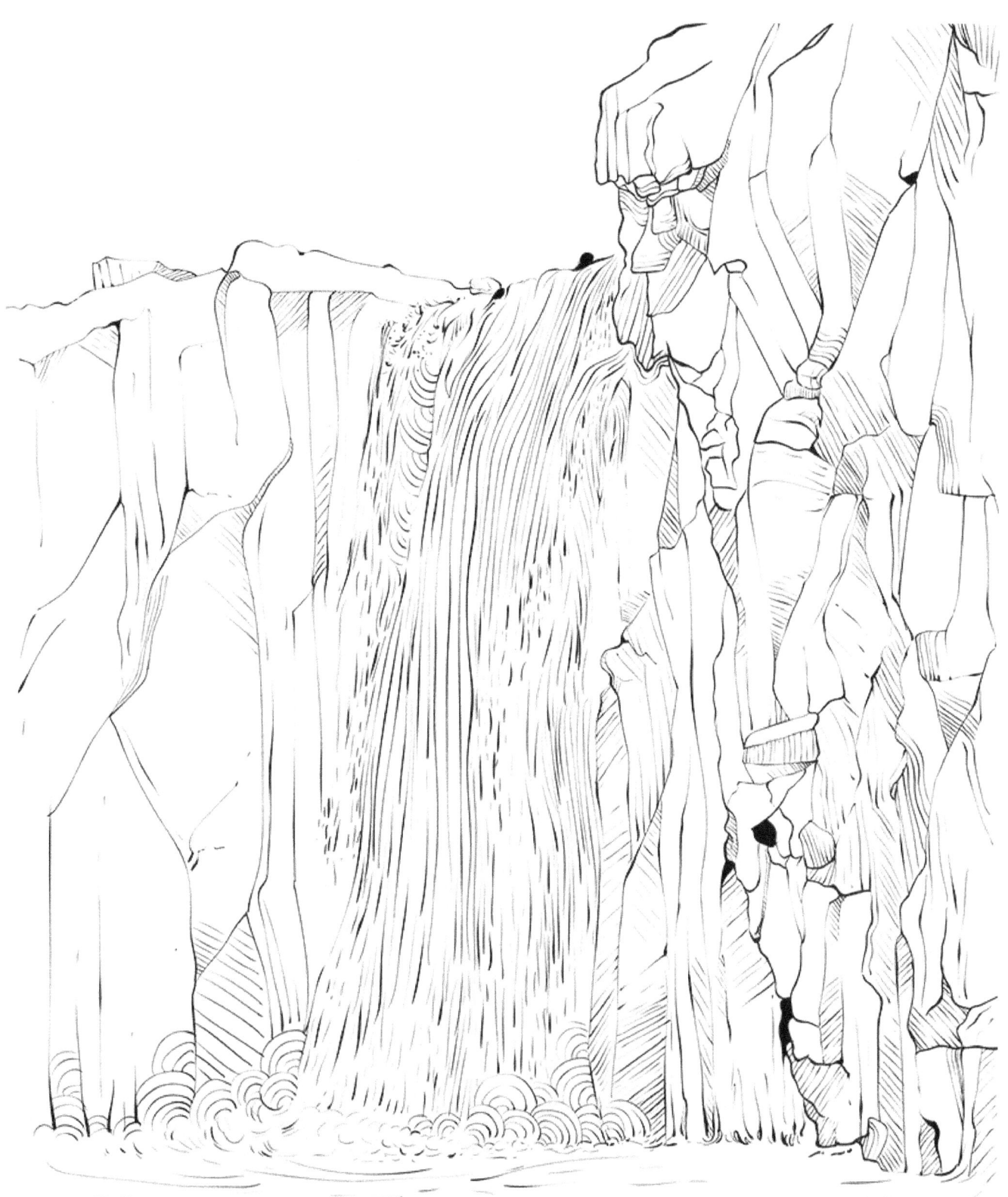

"Life does not start and stop at your convenience, you miserable piece of shit."

– Walter Sobchak (John Goodman) in The Big Lebowski

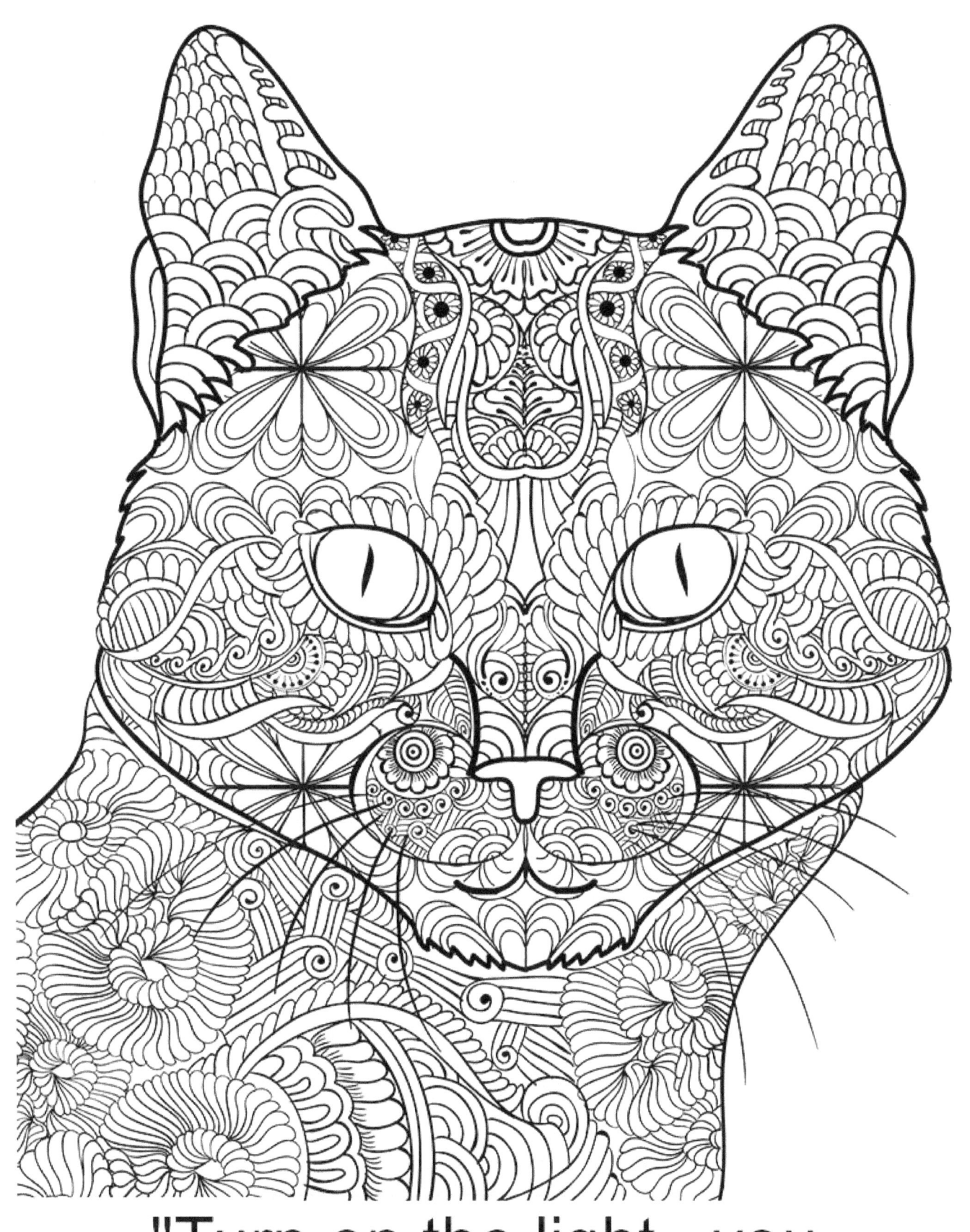

"Turn on the light , you
fucking dyke."   - Bound

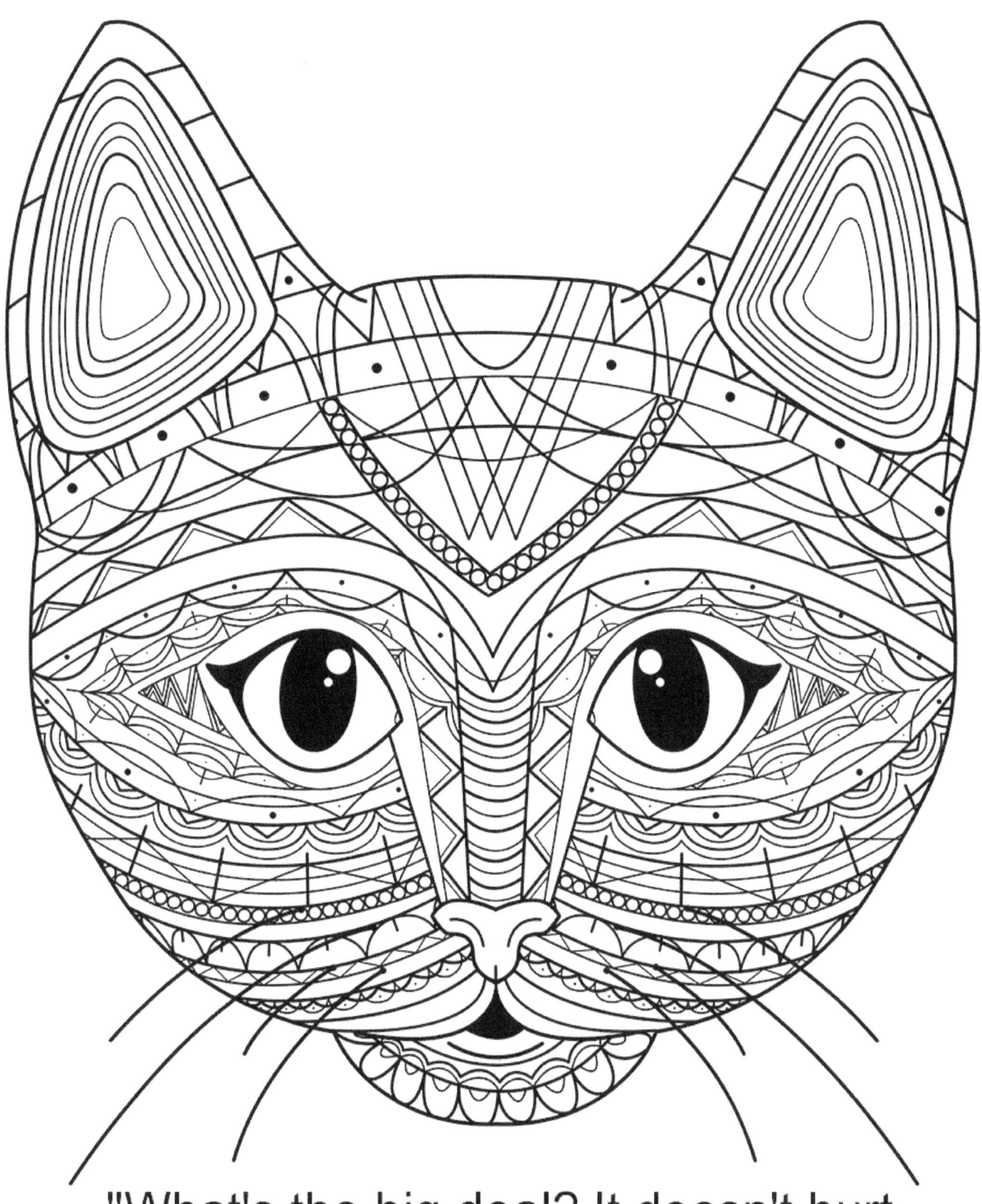

"What's the big deal? It doesn't hurt anybody. Fuck, fuckity, fuck-fuck-fuck!"

– Eric Cartman in South Park Bigger, Longer and Uncut

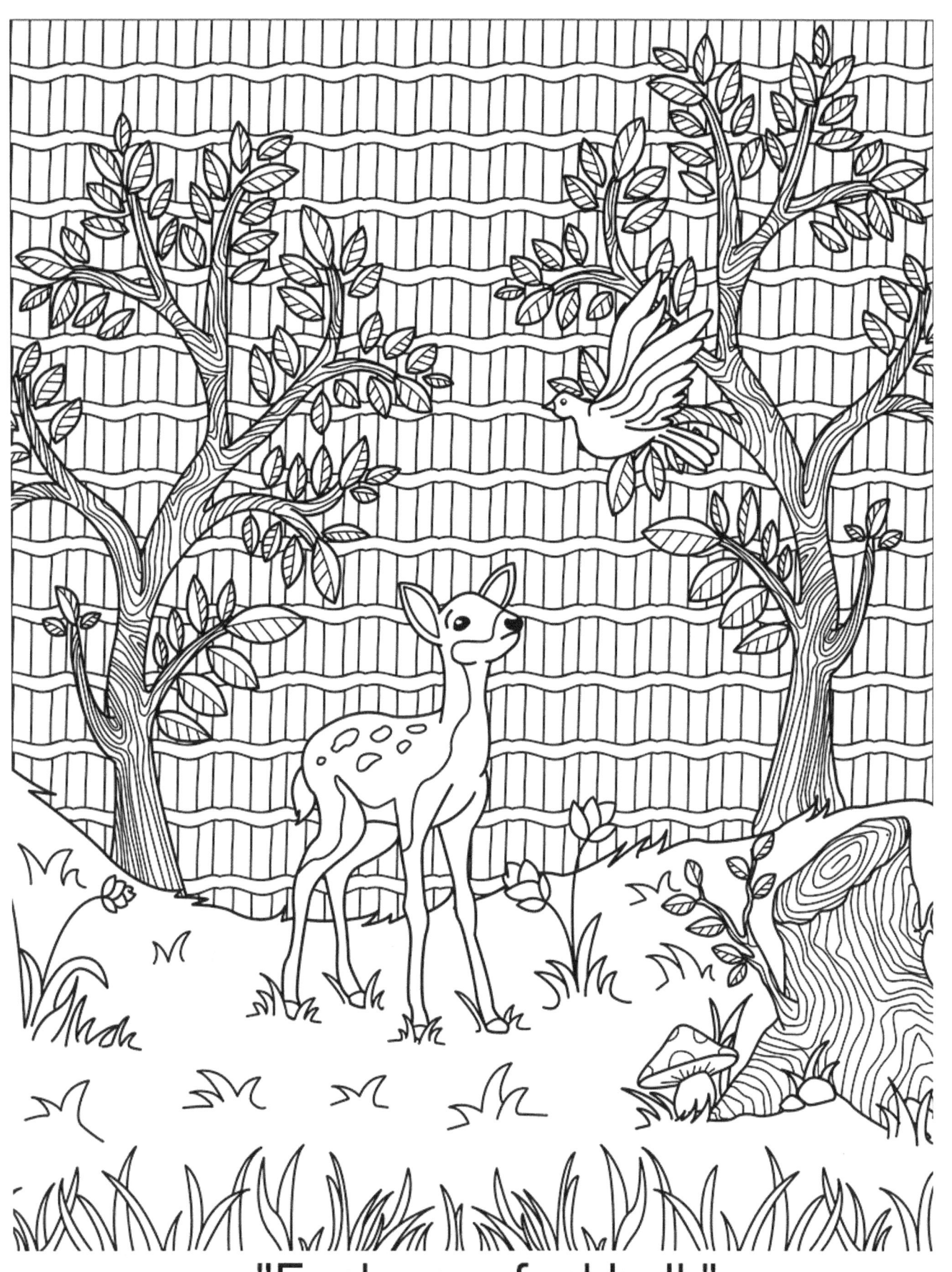

"Fuck you, fuckball."
- Get Shorty

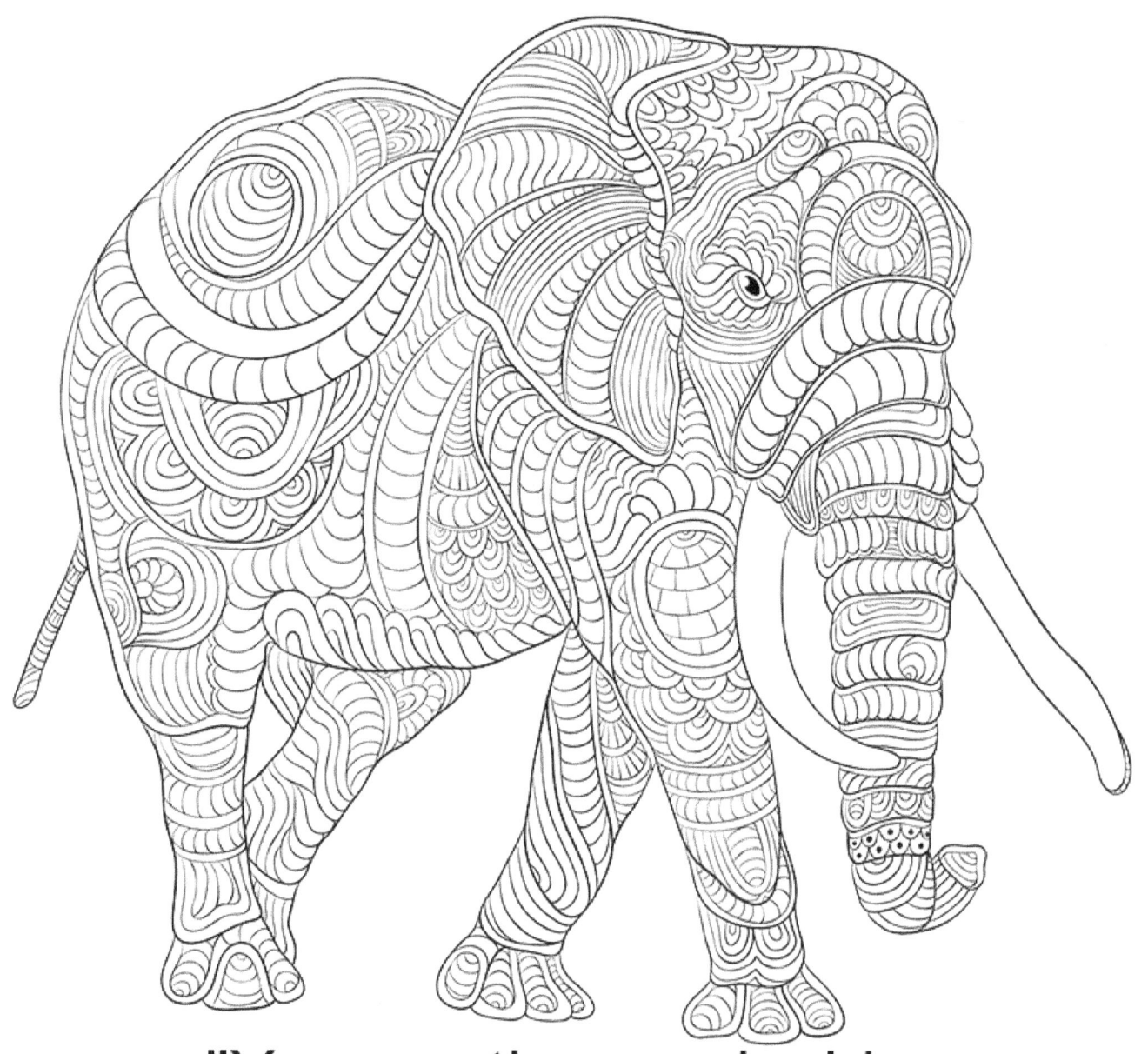

"Your mother sucks big fuckin' elephant dicks, you got that?"

– Joey LaMotta (Joe Pesci) in Raging Bull

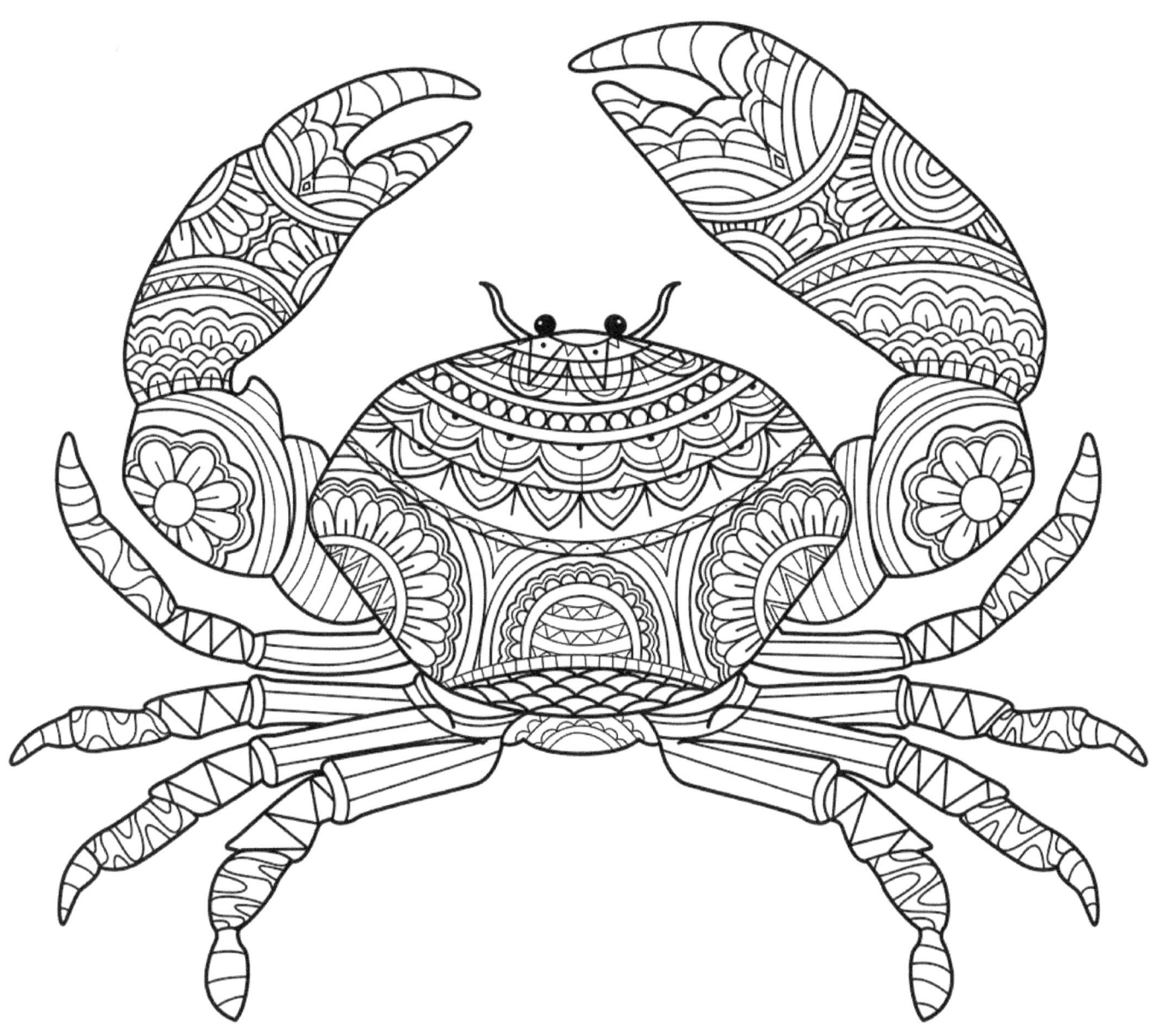

"Rick, I'm holding a do-I-give-a-shit-ometer in my hand, and the needle's not moving. Shut up."

— Douglas Coupland, Player One: What Is to Become of Us

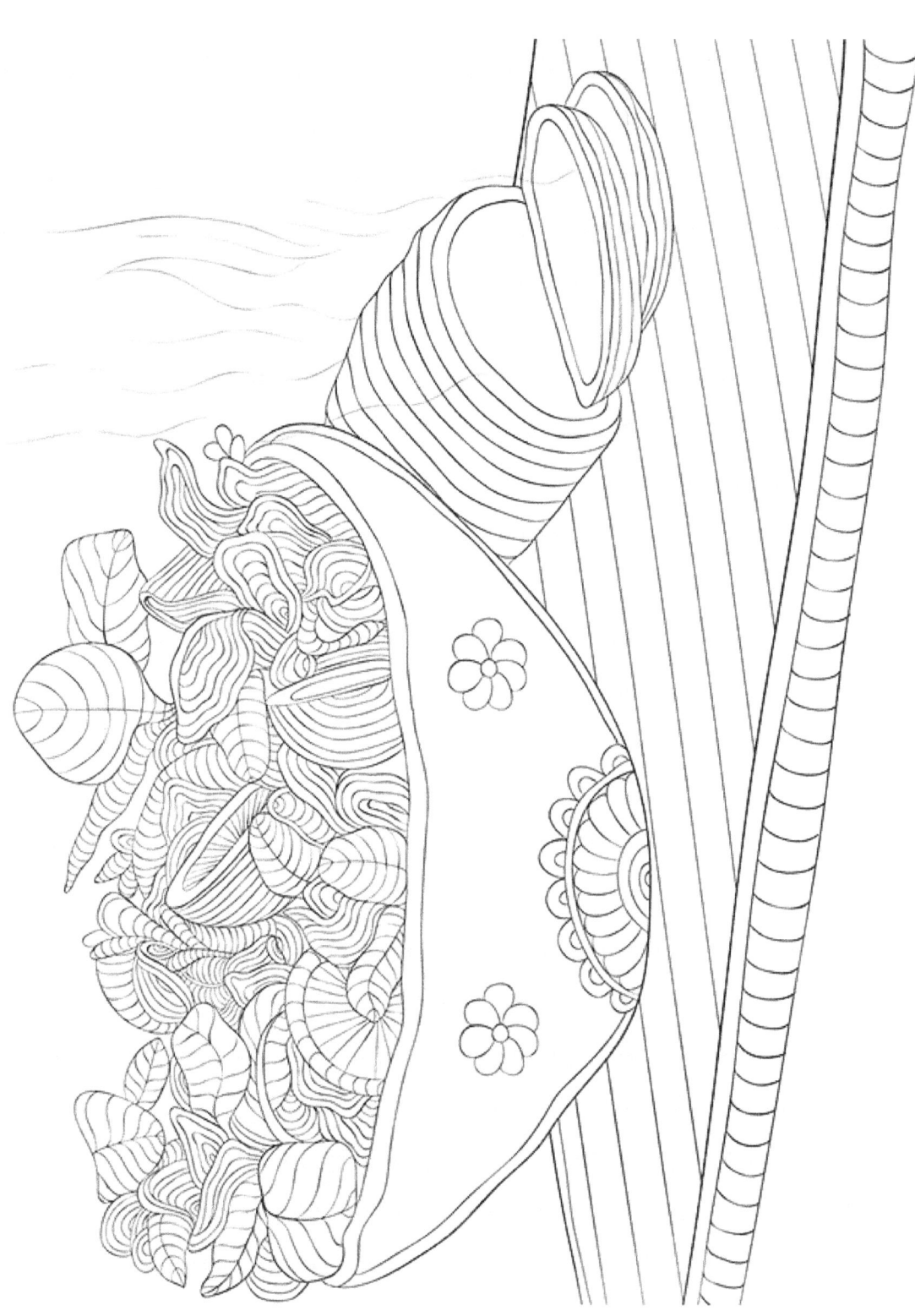

"Shit is the tofu of cursing and can be molded to whichever condition the speaker desires."

— David Sedaris

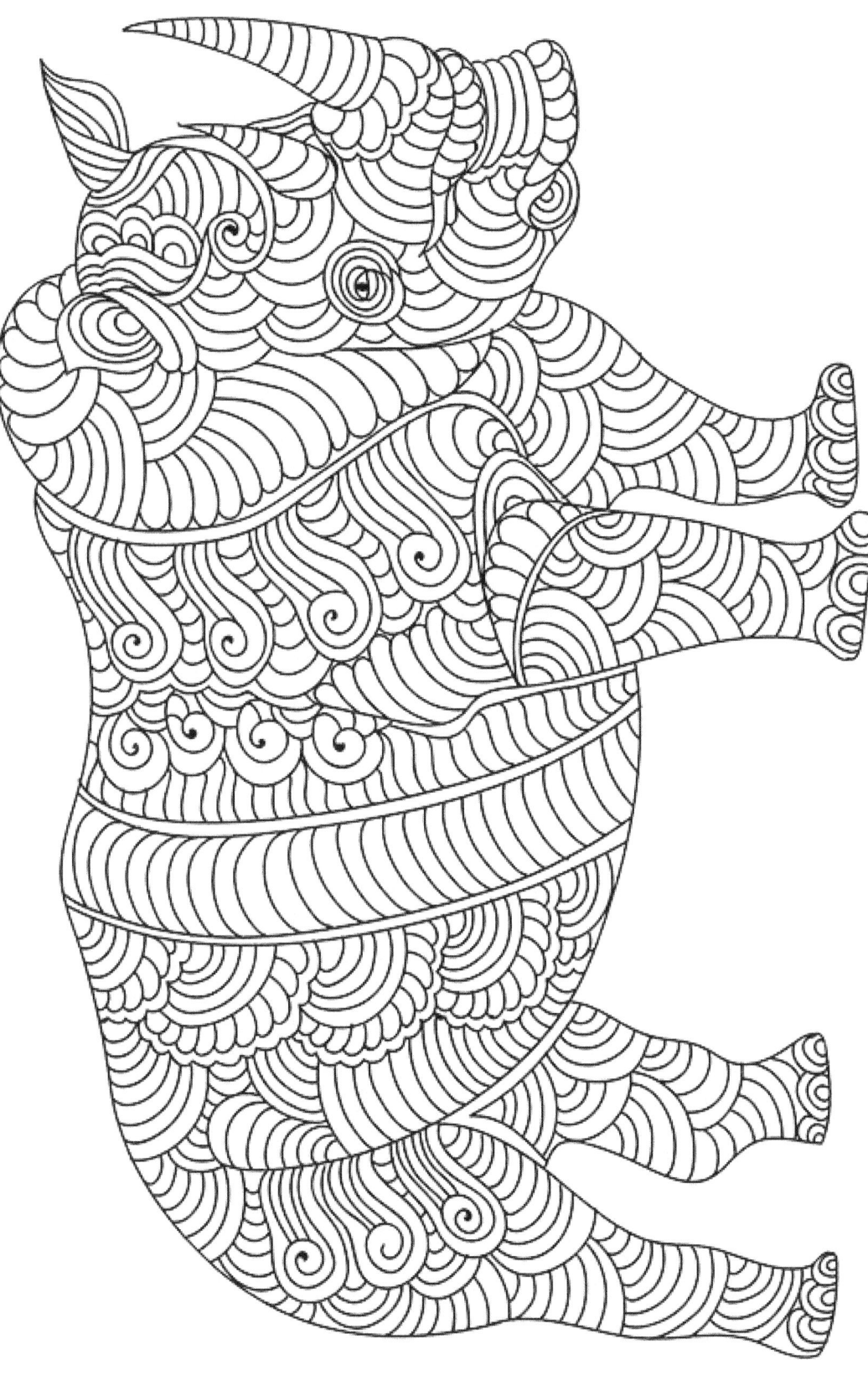

"Fuck a zombie!"
— Charlaine Harris, Dead in the Family

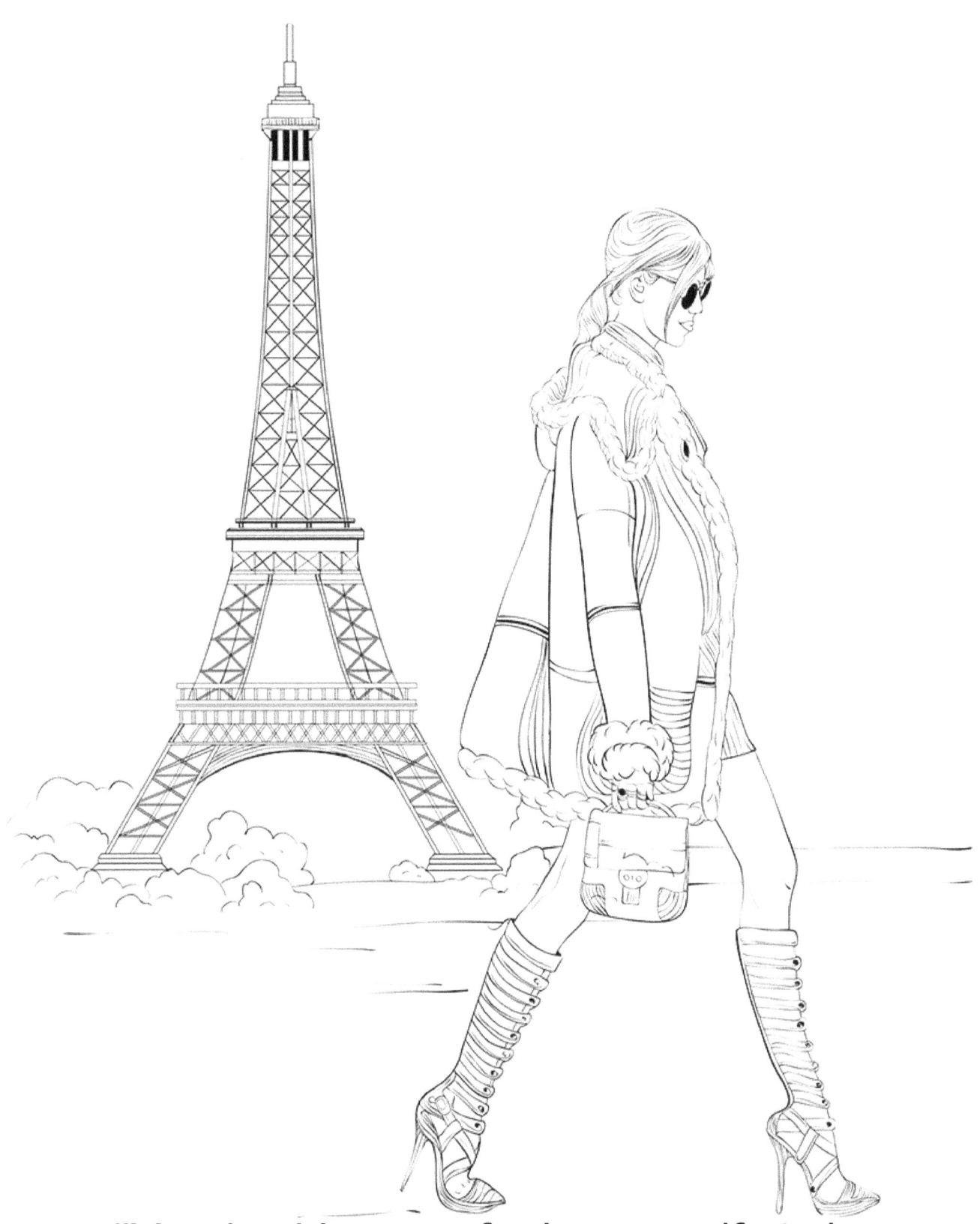

"You had best unfuck yourself and
start shitting me Tiffany cufflinks or I
will definitely fuck you up!"
– Gunnery Sergeant Hartman (Lee Ermey) in Full Metal Jacket

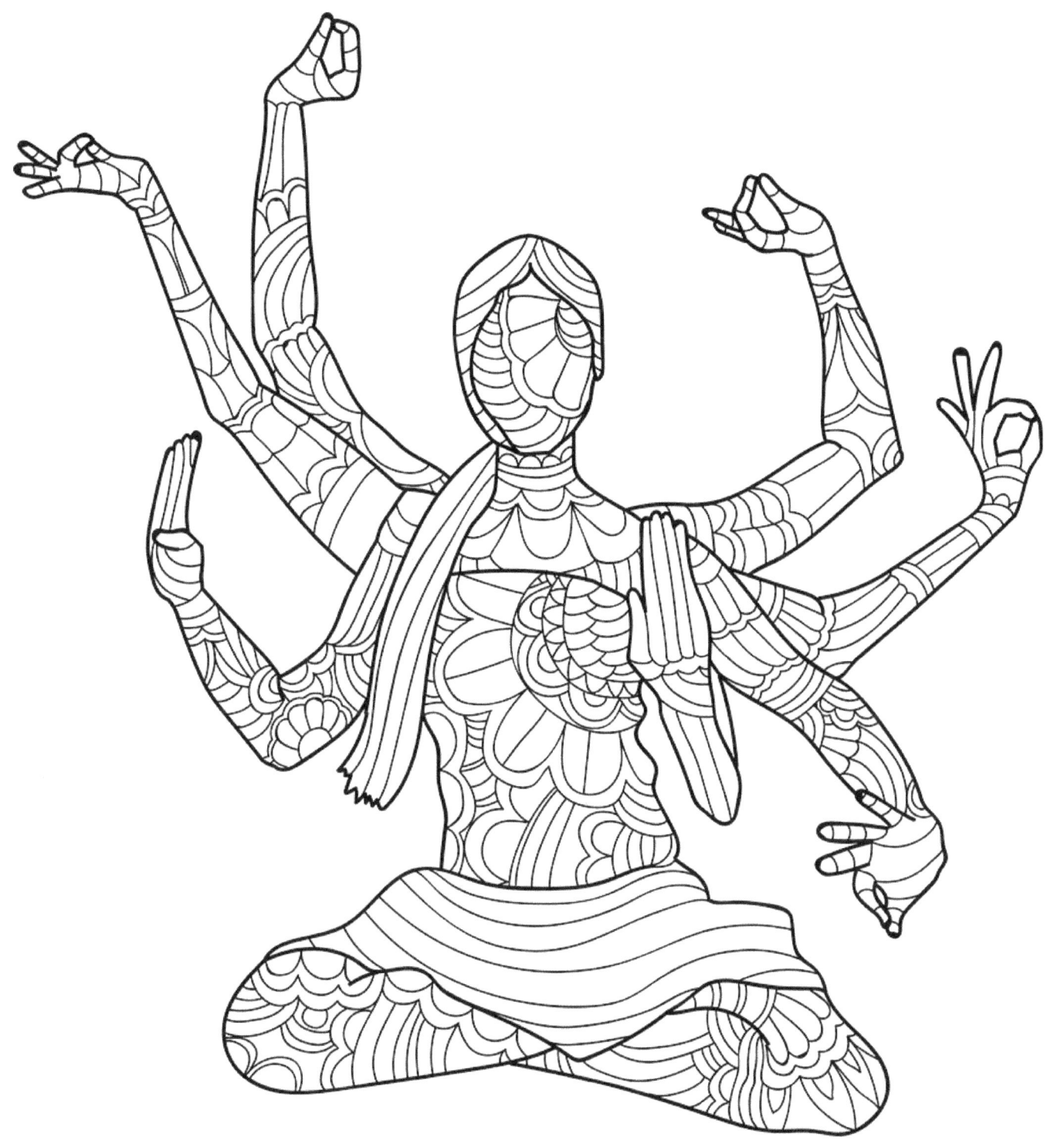

"I'm a heart surgeon, sure, but I'm just a mechanic. I go in and I fuck around and I fix things. Shit."

— Raymond Carver, Where I'm Calling From: New and Selected Stories

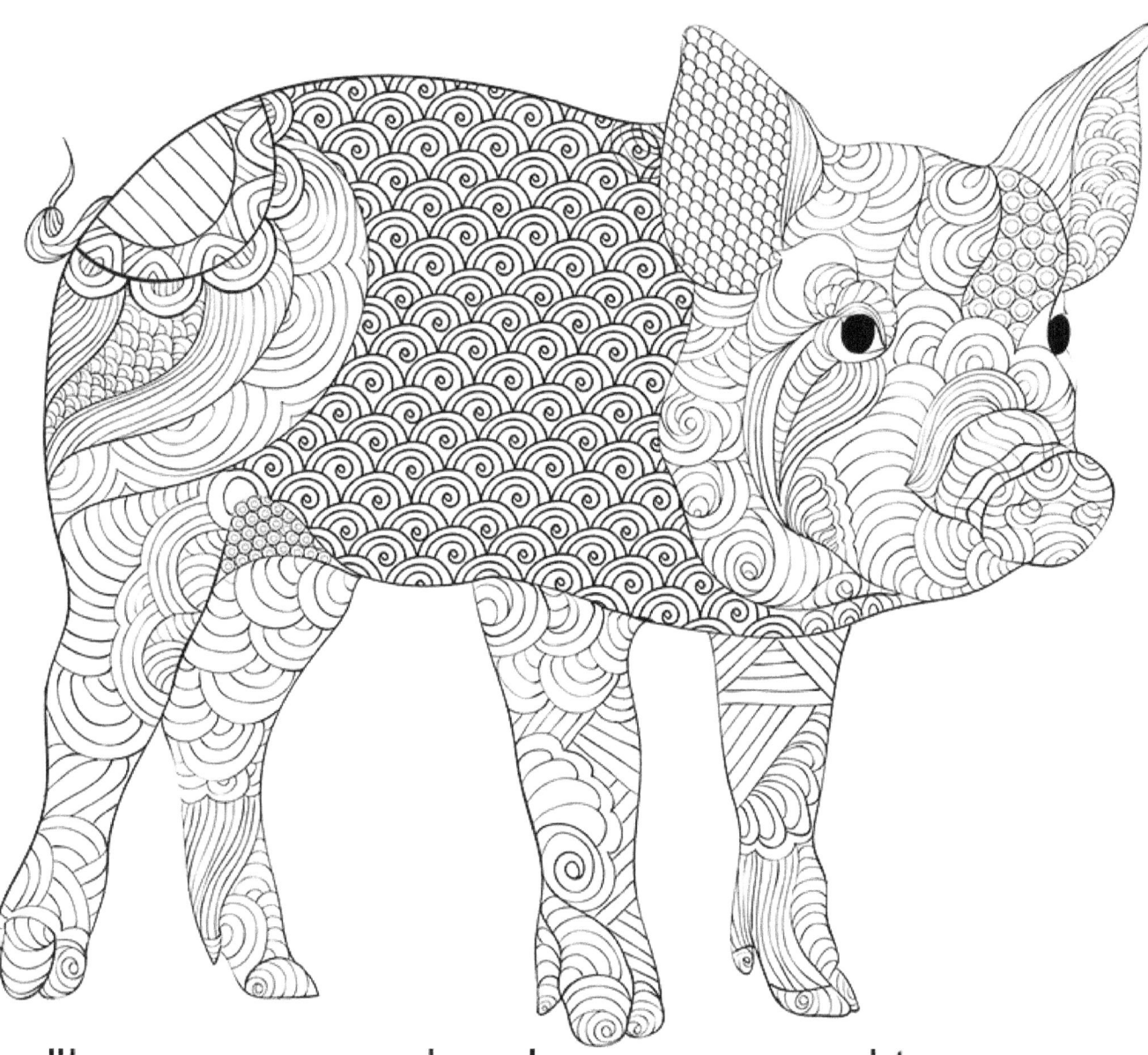

"In one scene, when I was supposed to say,
"In a pig's eye you are," what came out was,
"In a pig's ass you are." Old habits die awfully
hard."
— Ava Gardner, Ava: My Story

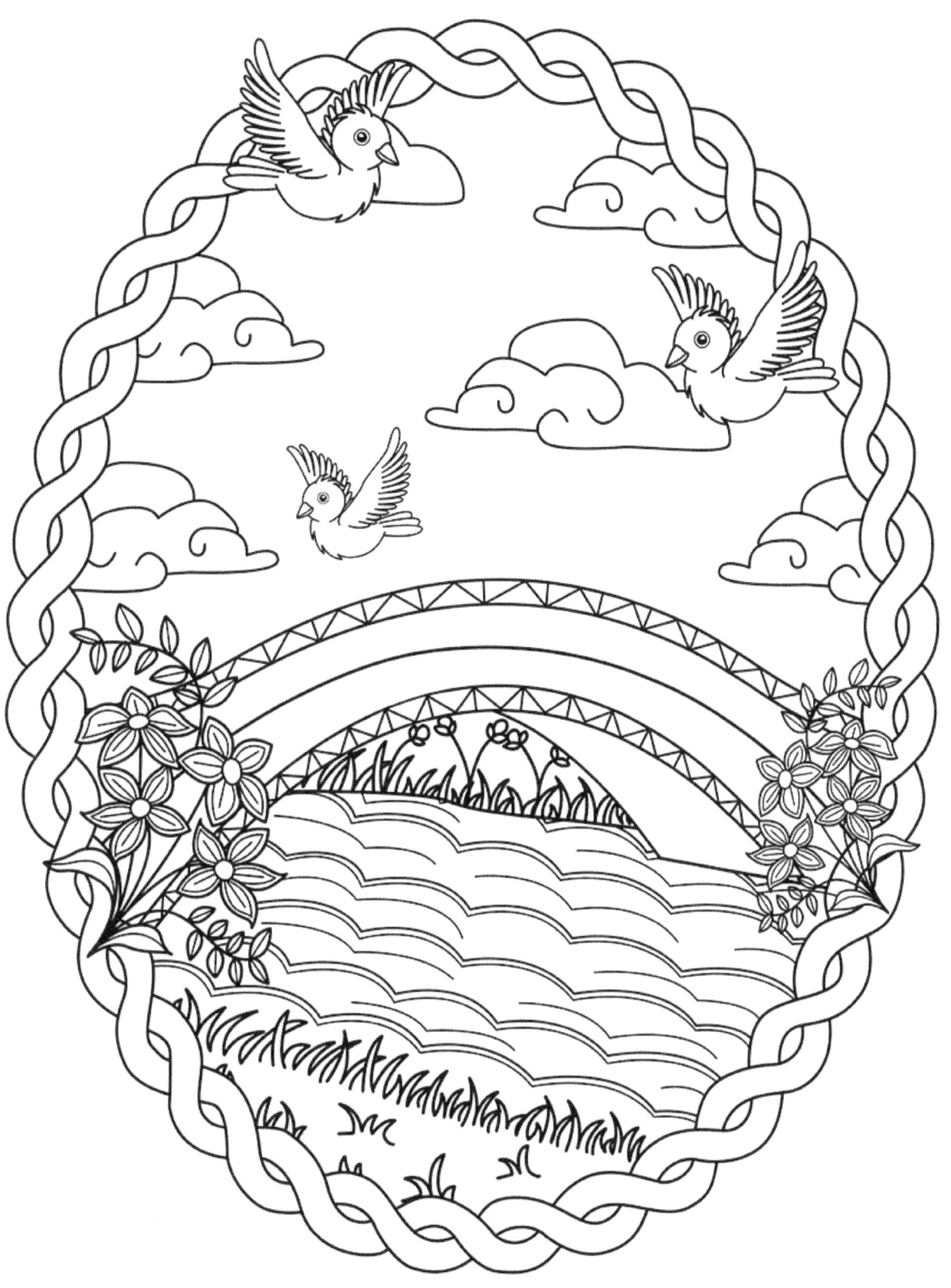

"Was it legal? FUCK legal! Not nice?
FUCK nice! The nation says I'm not nice?
FUCK THE NATION!"
– Roy Cohn (Al Pacino) in Angels in America

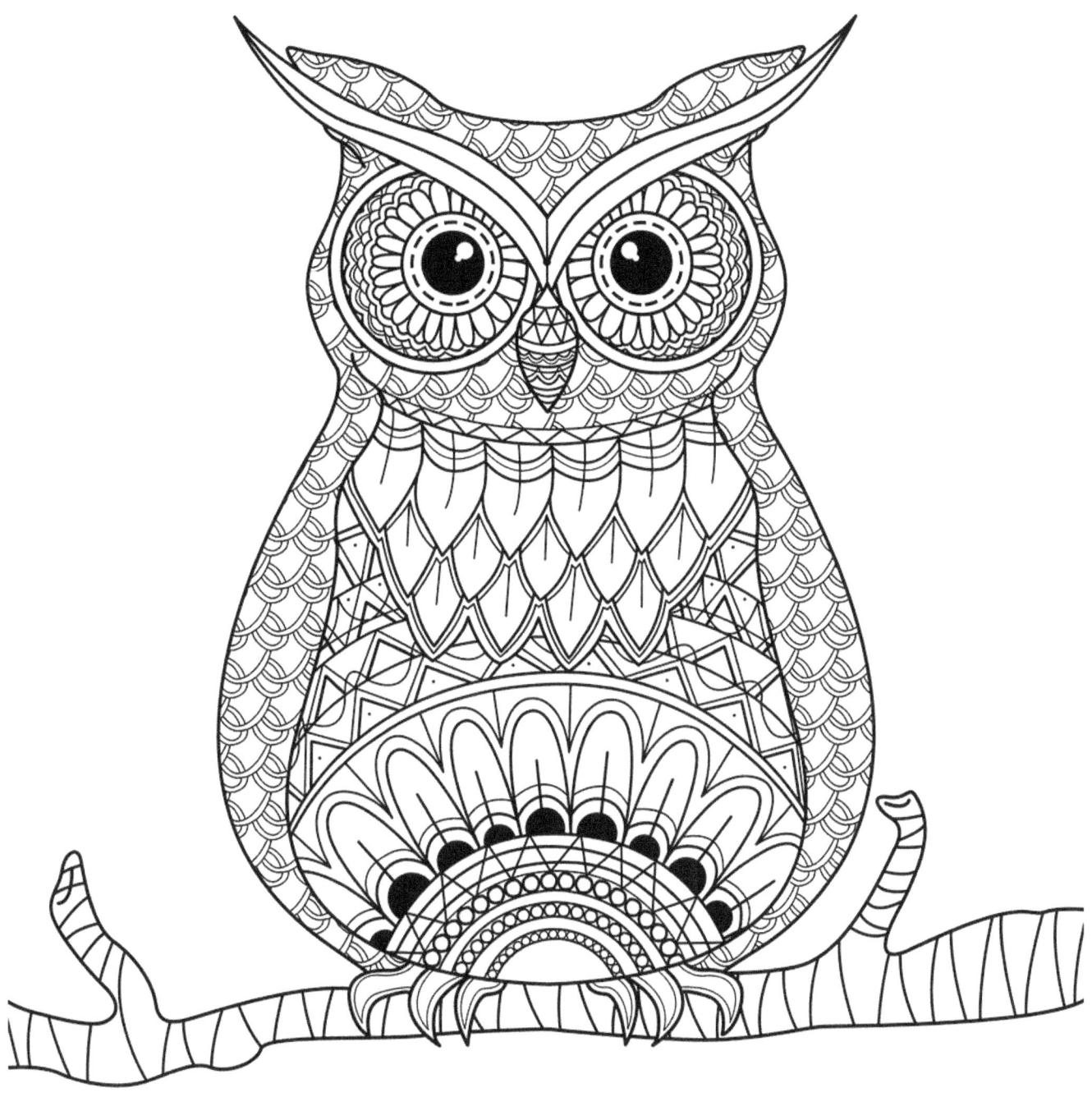

"And I know fuck isn't a word that Mormons
say, but I don't say this word I only think it,
so it doesn't really count."

— Sage Steadman "The Hippie", Snowflake Obsidian: Memoir of a Cutter

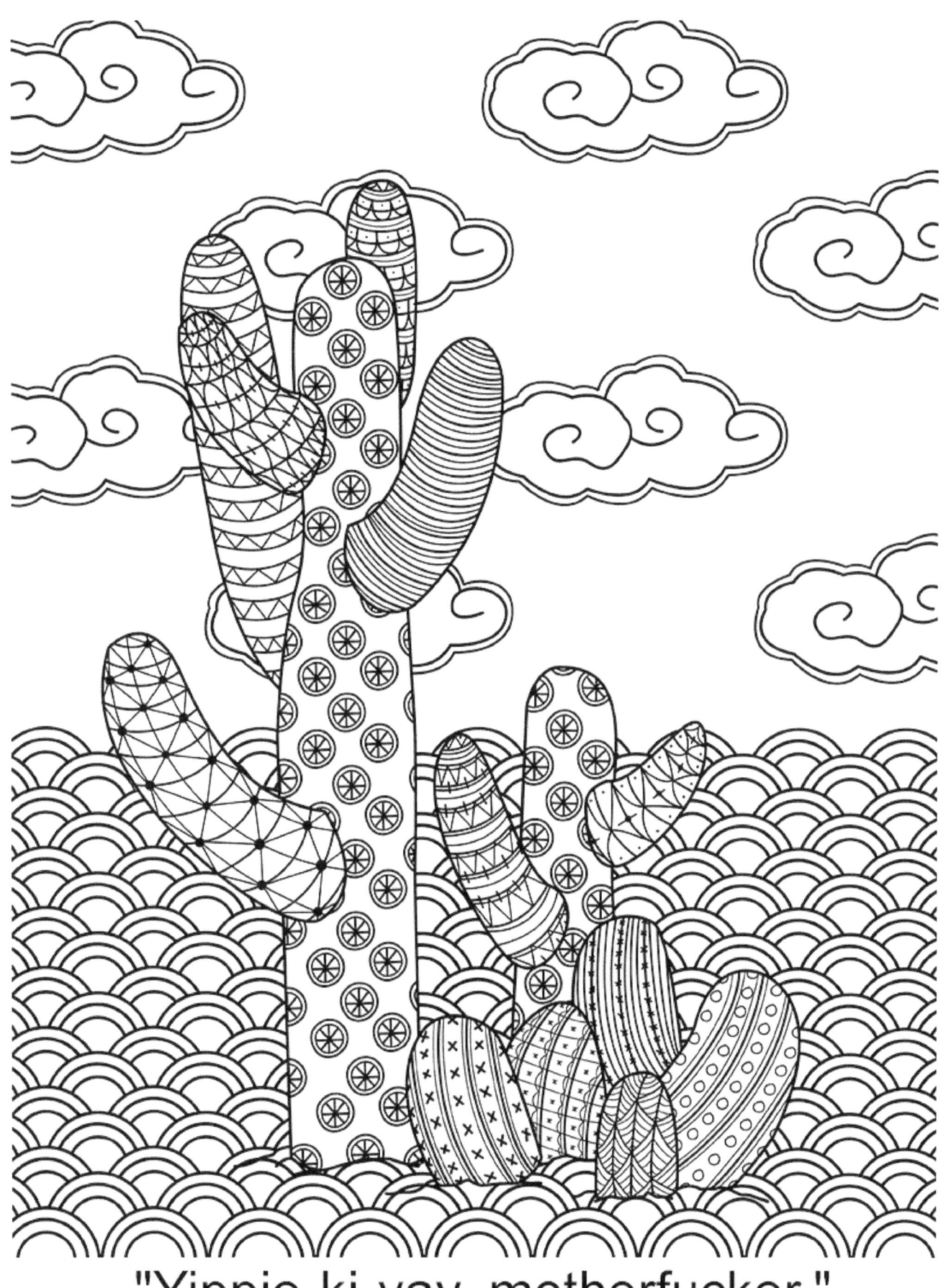

"Yippie-ki-yay, motherfucker."
- Die Hard

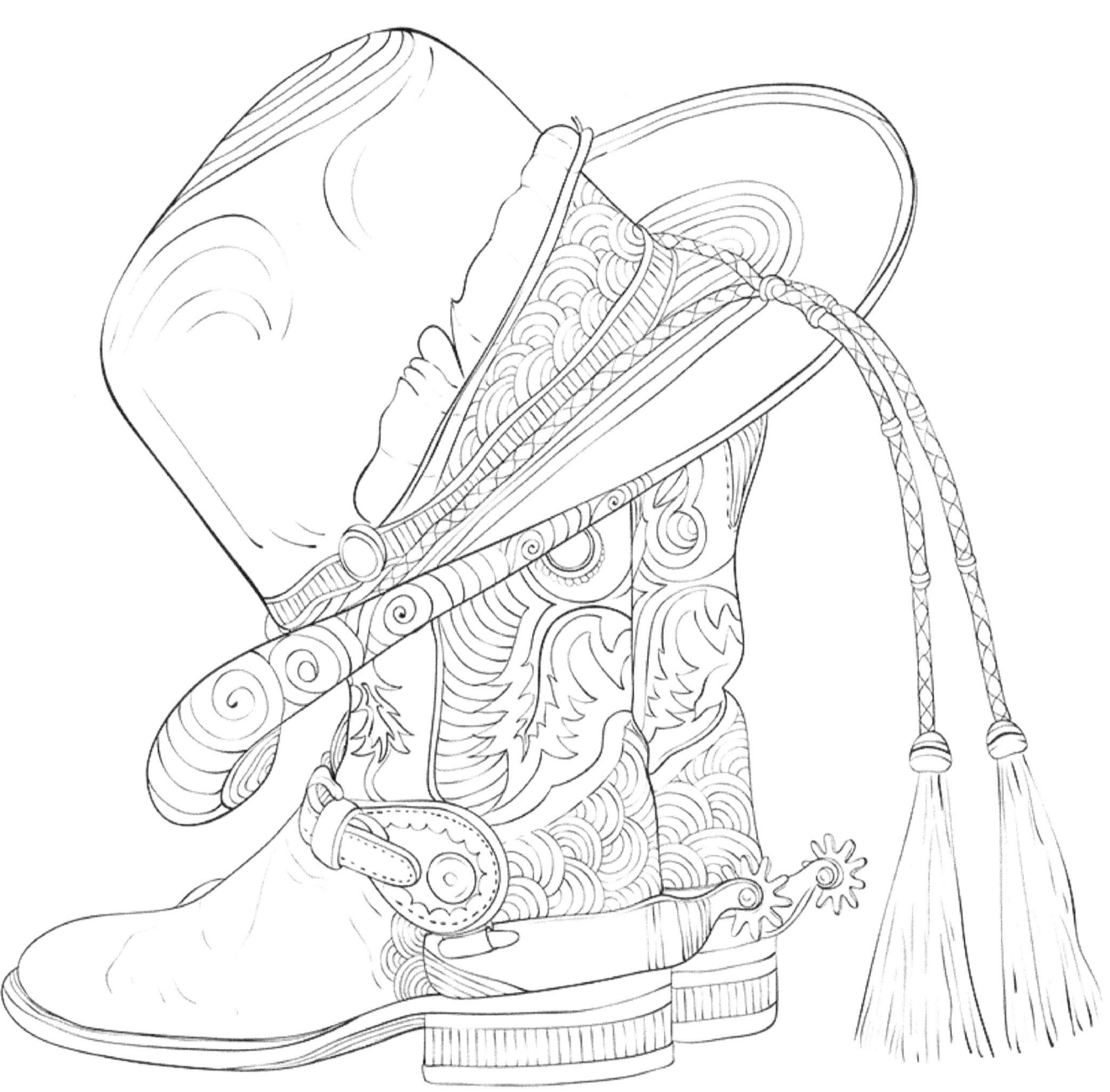

"Now go get your fucking shine box."
- Goodfellas

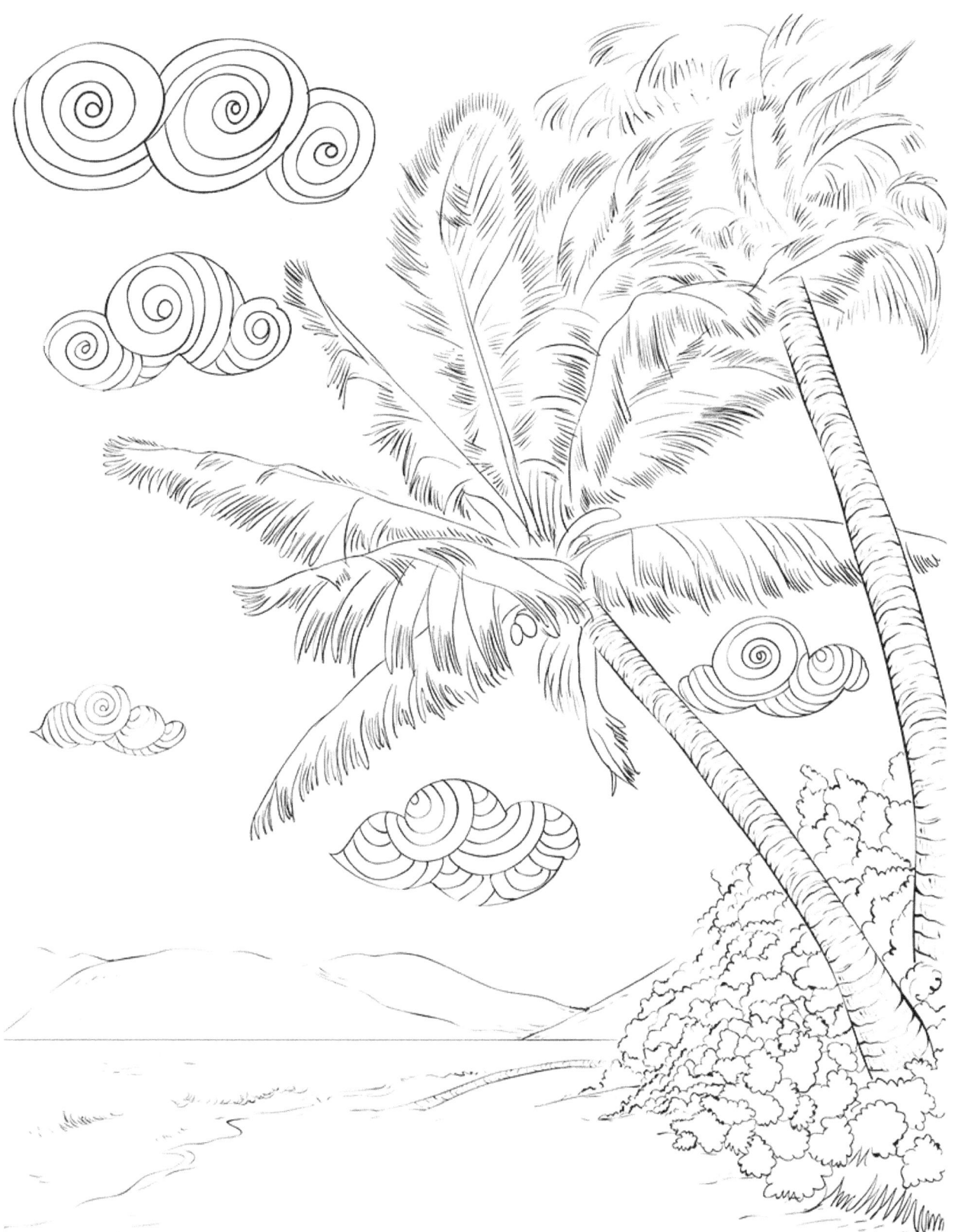

"So I say live and let live... Anyone who
can't go along with that, take him outside
and shoot the motherfucker."
– George Carlin

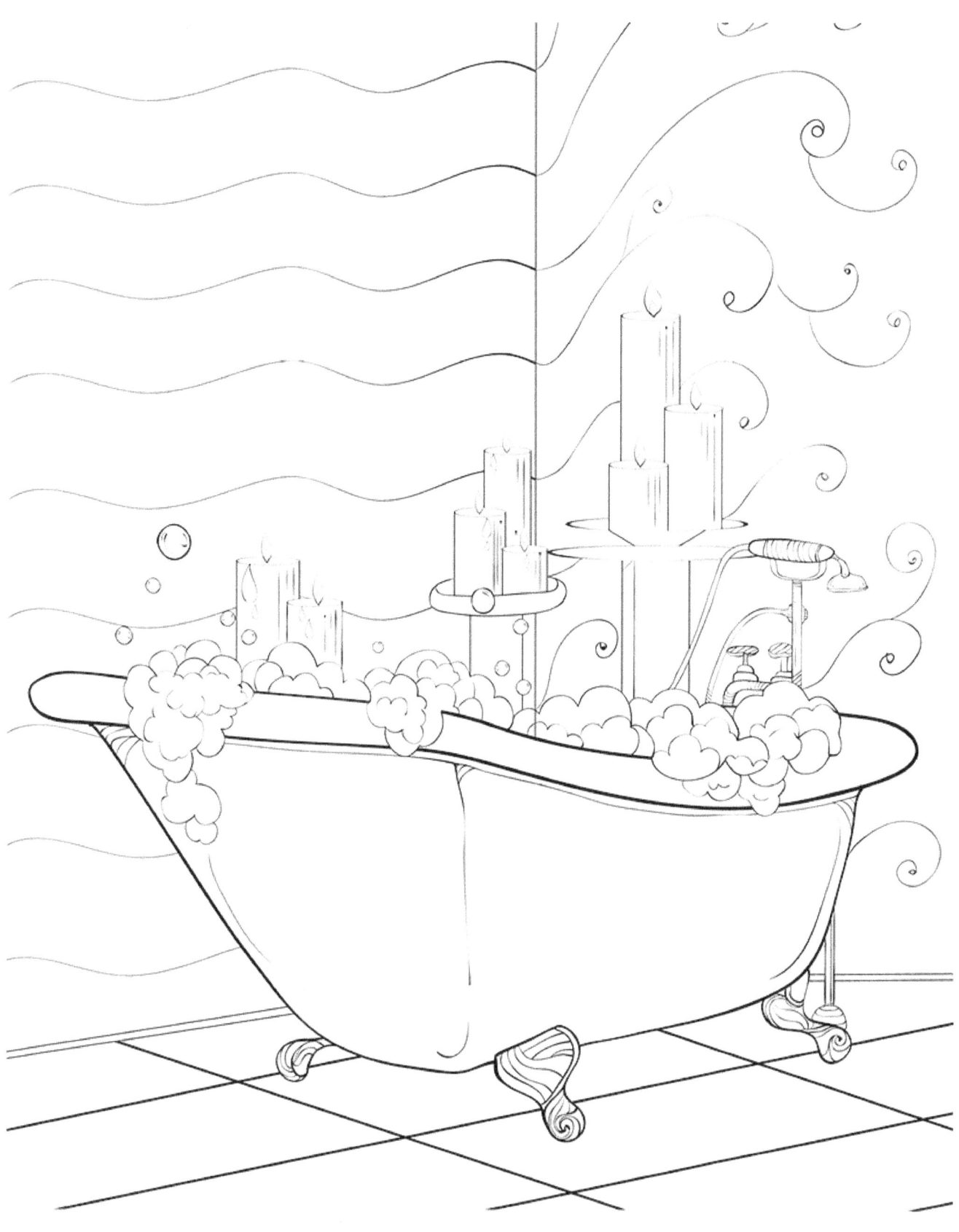

"Her pussy gets so wet."
- Election

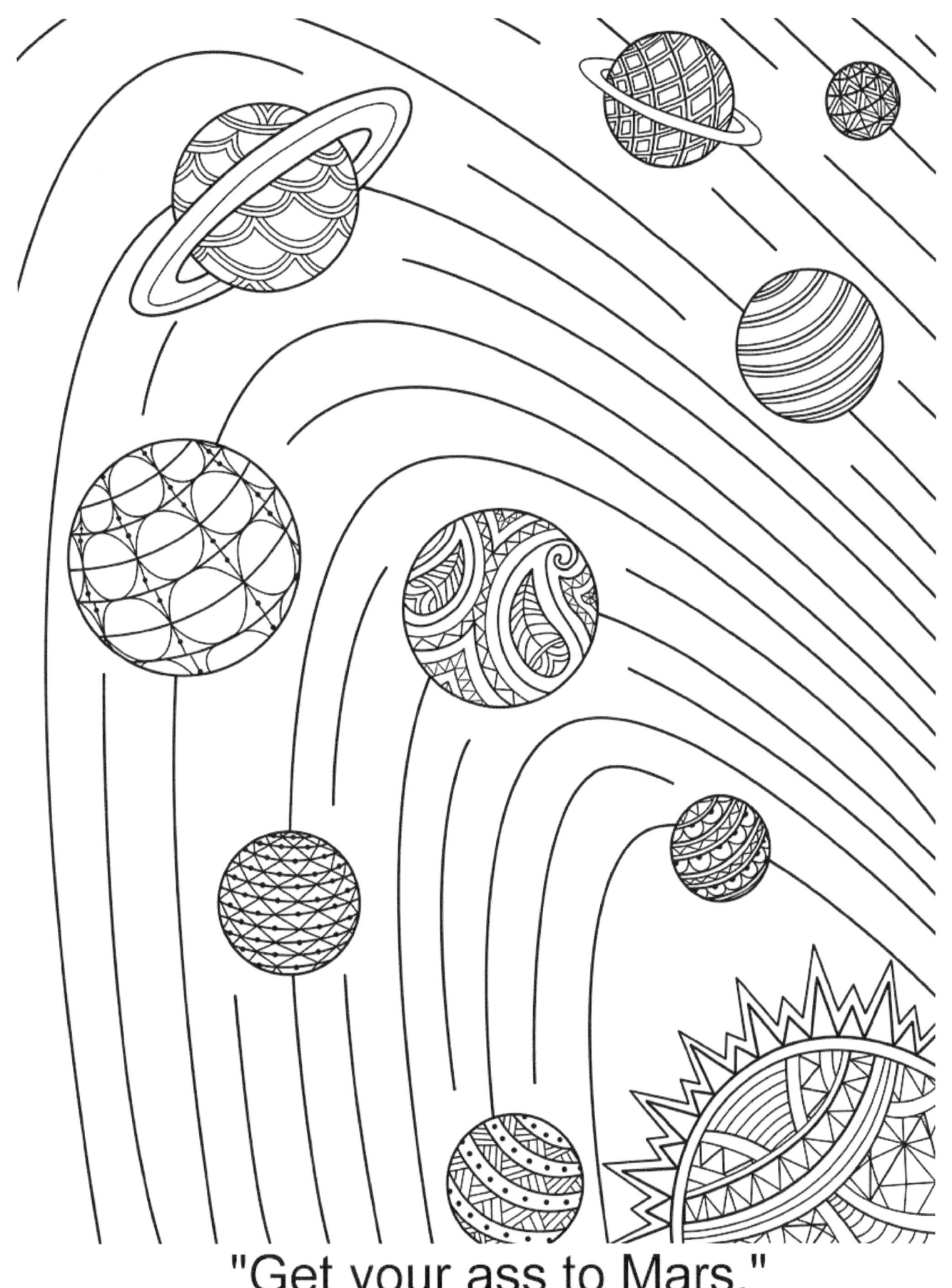

"Get your ass to Mars."
- Total Recall

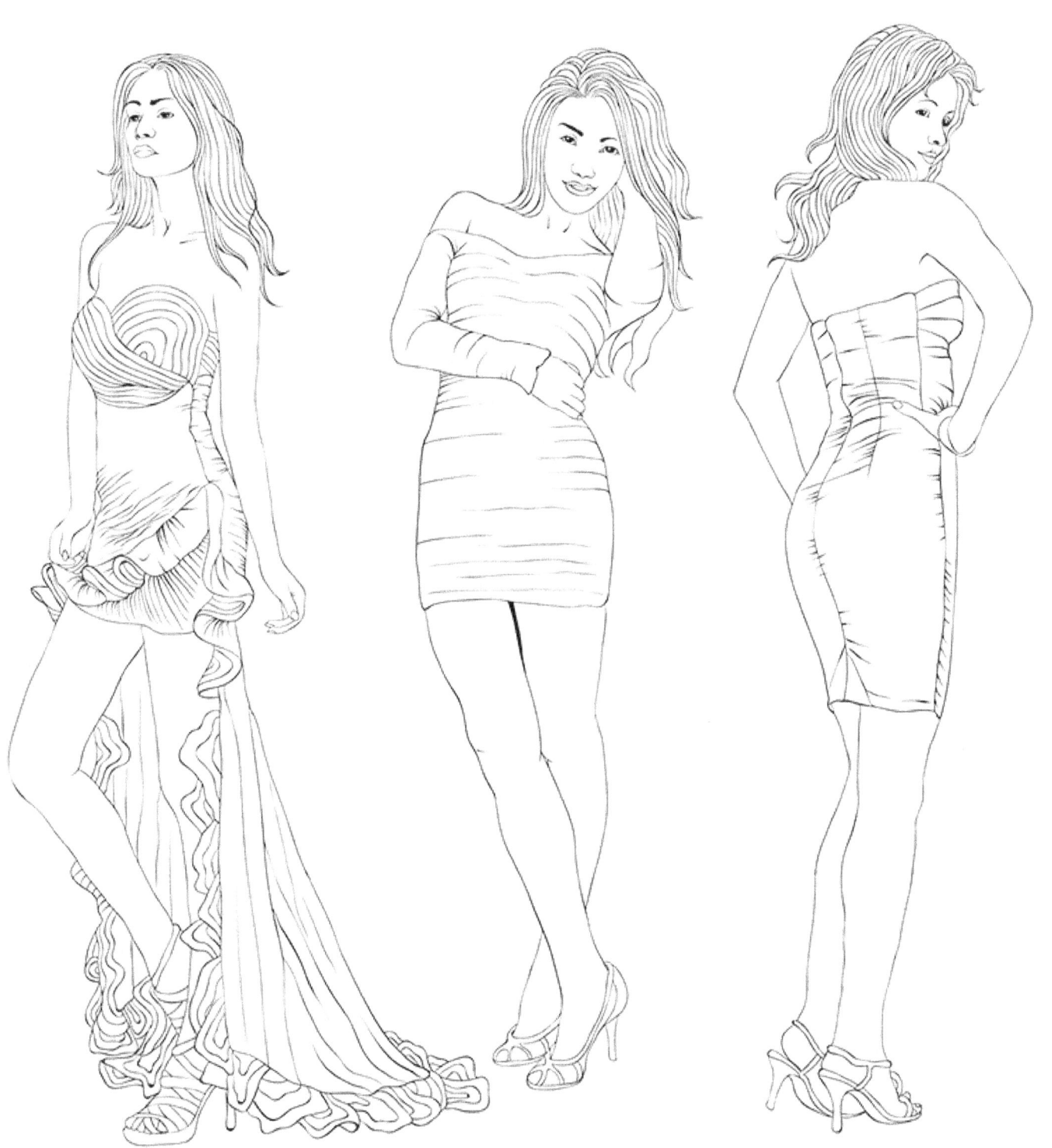

"I'll put your wife out on the street
to get fucked in the ass."
- Thief

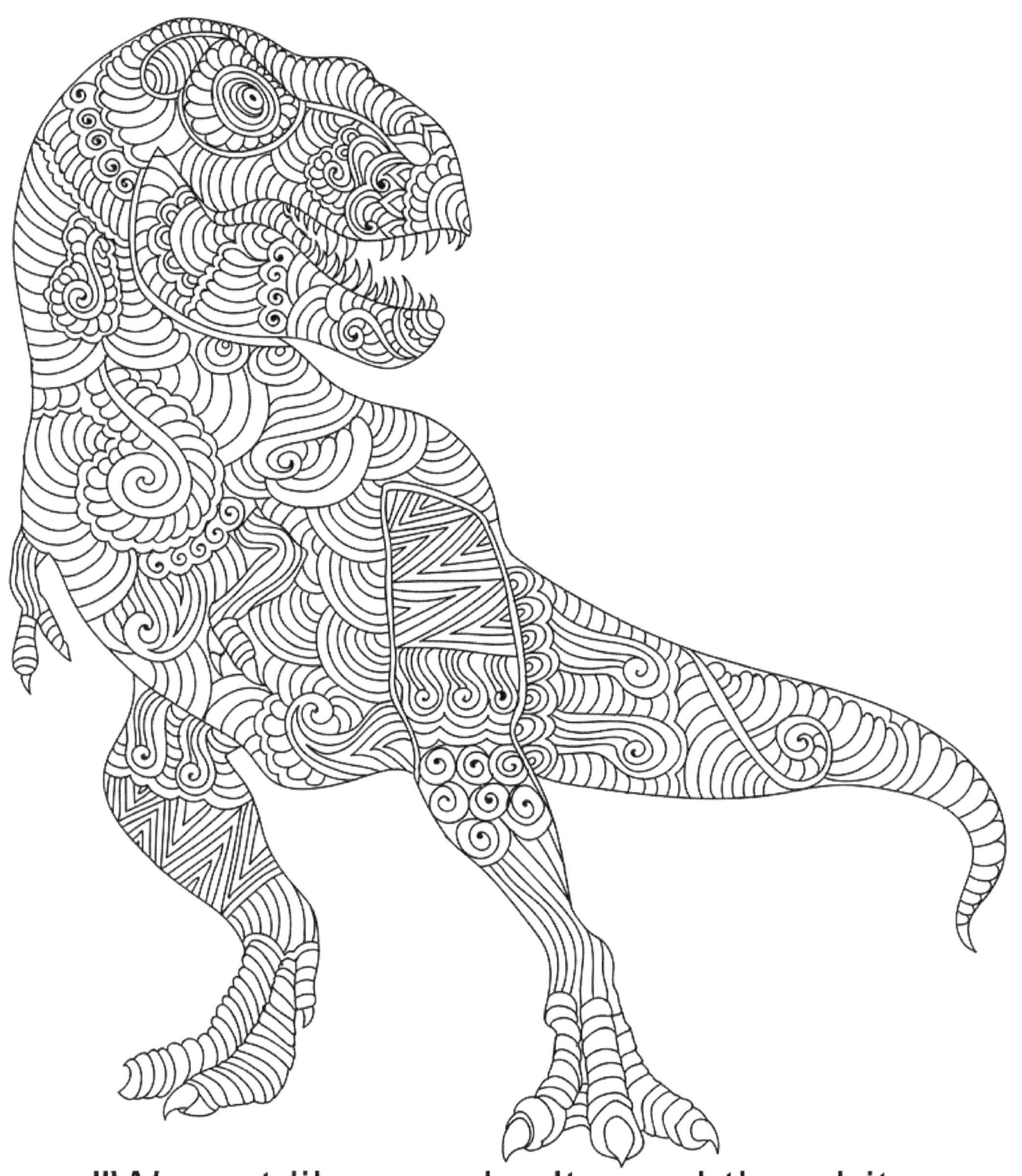

"We act like we don't need the shit,
they give us the shit for free."
- Swingers

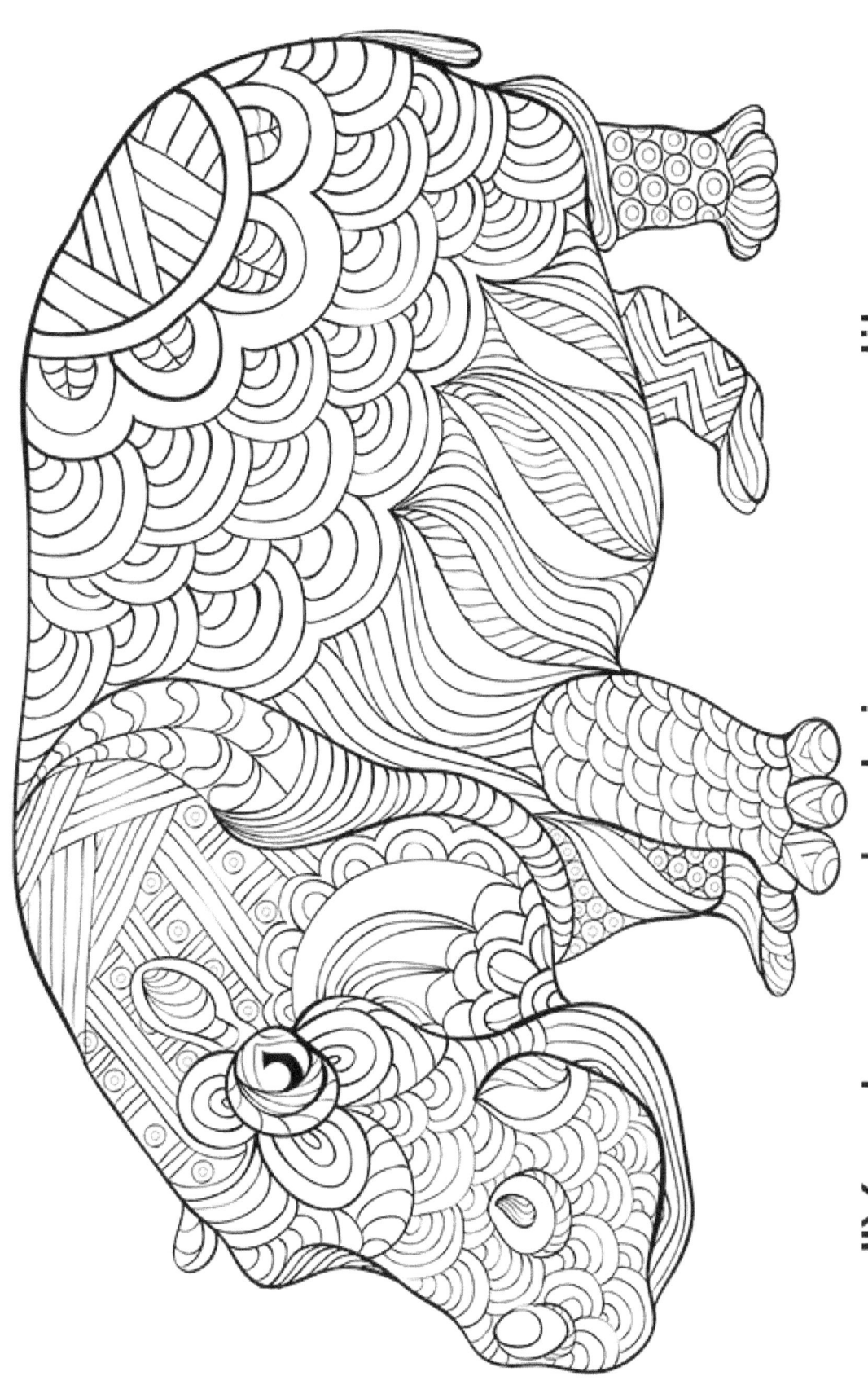

"You have a look in your eye like you haven't been fucked in a year."
— Tony Montana (Al Pacino) in Scarface

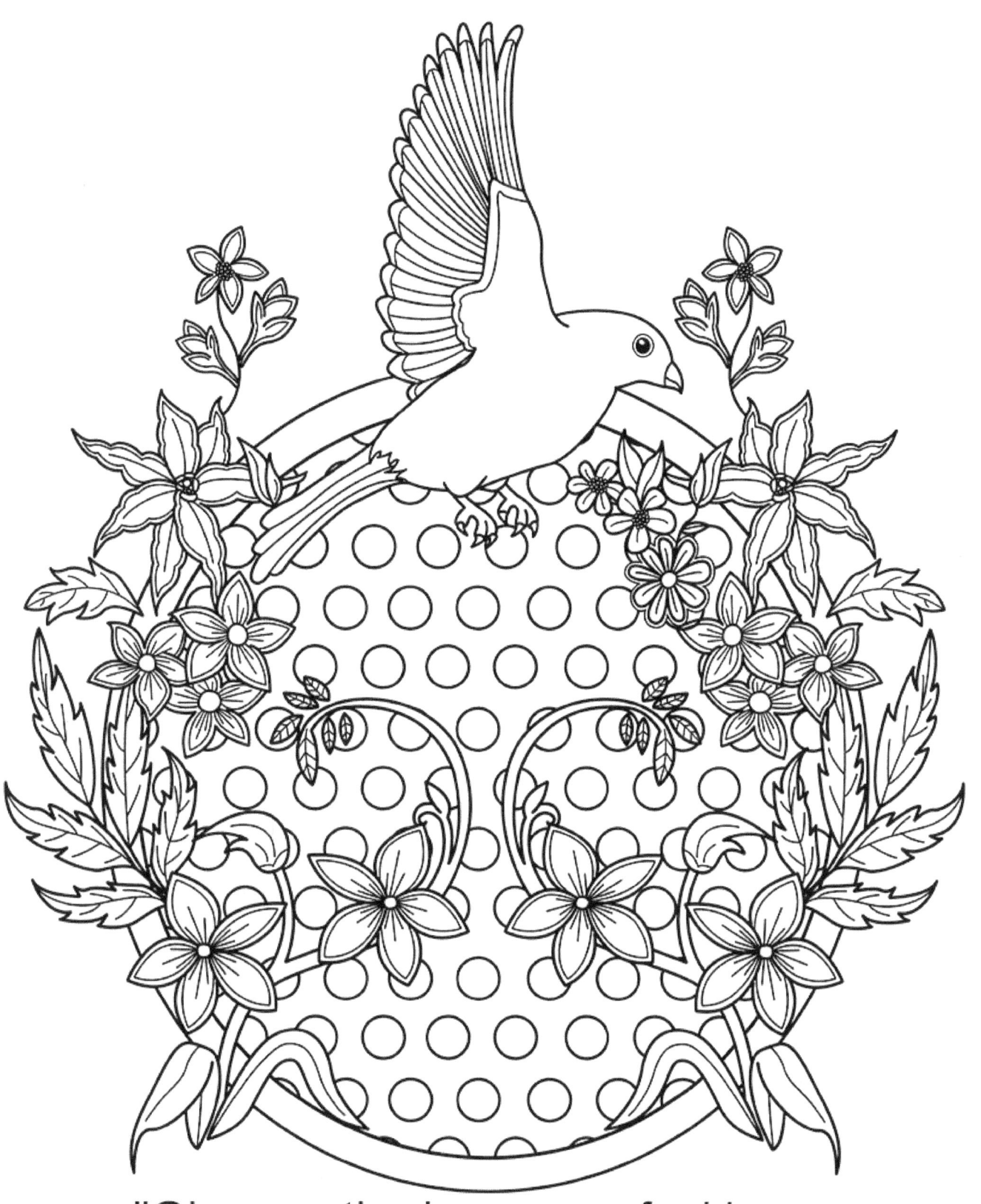

"Give me the keys, you fucking cocksucker."
- The Usual Suspects

www.ingramcontent.com/pod-product-compliance
Lightning Source LLC
Chambersburg PA
CBHW080640190526
45169CB00009B/3439